Argyll
& the Is

including Bute and Cowal

Photography by Colin Baxter

Text by Gilbert Summers

LOMOND BOOKS

EDINBURGH • SCOTLAND

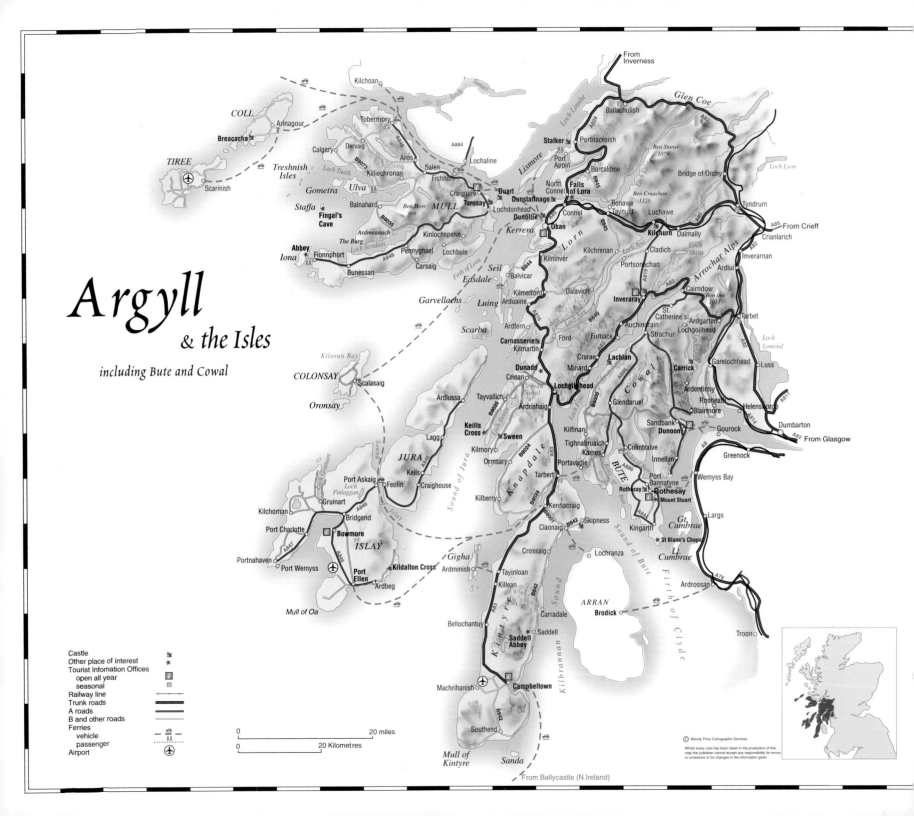

Argyll
& the Isles
including Bute and Cowal

Legend

Castle
Other place of interest
Tourist Information Offices
  open all year
  seasonal
Railway line
Trunk roads
A roads
B and other roads
Ferries
  vehicle
  passenger
Airport

0   20 miles
0   20 Kilometres

© Wendy Price Cartographic Services

Whilst every care has been taken in the production of this
map the publisher cannot accept any responsibility for errors
or omissions or for changes in the information given

Labels on map (selection):

From Inverness, Glen Coe, Ballachulish, A82, Loch Lyon, Loch Linnhe, Kilchoan, Loch Sunart, COLL, Annagour, TIREE, Scarinish, Breacacha, Calgary, Dervaig, Tobermory, Aros, A848, Salen, A884, Lochaline, Lismore, Port Appin, Stalker, Portnacroish, Ben Starav 1079, B845, Barcaldine, North Connel, Falls of Lora, Bridge of Orchy, Ben Cruachan 1126, Treshnish Isles, Gometra, Ulva, Killiechronan, Fishnish, Craignure, Duart, Dunstaffnage, Bonawe, Taynuilt, Lochawe, Tyndrum, Staffa, Fingal's Cave, Ben More 966, MULL, Torosay, Lochdonhead, Dunollie, Connel, Oban, Kilchurn, Dalmally, A85, From Crieff, Crianlarich, The Burg, Ardmeanach, Loch Scridain, Kinlochspelve, Kerrera, Kilchrenan, Cladich, Portsonachan, Inverarnan, Abbey, Iona, Fionnphort, Pennyghael, Lochbuie, A849, Kilninver, Loch Awe, Arrochar Alps, Ardlui, A82, Bunessan, Carsaig, Seil, Easdale, Balvicar, Kilmelford, Dalavich, Ben Ime 1011, Cairndow, Tarbet, Garvellachs, Luing, Scarba, Arduaine, Ardfern, Ford, Furnace, Inveraray, St. Catherine's, Ardgartan, Lochgoilhead, Loch Lomond, Carnasserie, Kilmartin, Crarae, Minard, Lachlan, Cowal, Carrick, Garelochhead, Luss, Kiloran Bay, COLONSAY, Scalasaig, Dunadd, Crinan, Lochgilphead, Crinan Canal, Glendaruel, Ardentinny, Rosneath, Helensburgh, Oronsay, Ardlussa, Tayvallich, Ardrishaig, Kilfinan, Tighnabruaich, Kames, Sandbank, Dunoon, Gourock, Greenock, Lagg, Keills Cross, Sween, Kilmory, Ormsary, Portavadie, Innellan, Colintraive, BUTE, Port Bannatyne, Wemyss Bay, JURA, Keils, Craighouse, Kilberry, Tarbert, Rothesay, Mount Stuart, Largs, Port Askaig, Feolin, Kennacraig, Gt. Cumbrae, Kilchoman, Gruinart, Bridgend, Claonaig, Skipness, Kingarth, St Blane's Chapel, Port Charlotte, Bowmore, ISLAY, Crossaig, Lochranza, Lt. Cumbrae, Portnahaven, Port Wemyss, Kildalton Cross, Gigha, Ardminish, Tayinloan, ARRAN, Brodick, Ardrossan, Port Ellen, Ardbeg, Mull of Oa, Killean, Carradale, Troon, Bellochantuy, Kintyre, Saddell, Saddell Abbey, Machrihanish, Campbeltown, Southend, Mull of Kintyre, Sanda, From Ballycastle (N.Ireland), Firth of Clyde, From Glasgow

Argyll & the Isles

including Bute and Cowal

CONTENTS

Argyll & the Isles

Introduction

The indented, tortuous nature of Scotland's western seaboard is nowhere at its more complex than where it makes up the western edge of Argyll. This grand swathe of Scottish landscape meets the central Highlands around Loch Lomond to the east, and the northern Highlands – or, at least, Lochaber – south of Glencoe. Virtually all of Argyll lies above the Highland Line or Highland Boundary Fault, the very real geological boundary between Highland and Lowland.

However, with its complicated sea passages and scattering of islands, if Argyll has one characteristic above all others it is the nearness of mountain and sea to each other. Fjord-like sea lochs indent the coastline deeply, sending long fingers of salt water far into the wild country of the west. These same lochs add a picturesque quality for the tourer – and extra miles for the traveller in a hurry!

Essentially, Argyll is not an area to hurry through. Around a hundred miles (160 km) separates the north end of Mull from the south tip of Kintyre, and more than sixty (96 km) from the head of Loch Fyne westwards to Iona, so that the area is also large enough to have many special and characteristic landscapes within it. Argyll embraces both the soft green fields of the south end of the island of Bute (actually below the Highland Line) and the shattered rocky ridges of high Ben Cruachan, guarding the approaches to Oban through the Pass of Brander by way of Loch Awe. Similarly, the area includes both the dairy pastures of

Kintyre around Campbeltown and the empty reaches of the deer forests of the island of Jura. To the south-east, but not included in this guide, are the Rosneath Peninsula and the lands east of Gare Loch, from Helensburgh on the Firth of Clyde to Luss on Loch Lomond.

Argyll lies at the core of Scotland's own story. The ancient kingdom of Dalriada was founded here by around AD 500, settled by Celtic peoples known as Scots. They came from Ulster, across the North Channel. Their power base lay at Dunadd, a rocky rounded hill not far from Crinan. The indented coastline became the sea-lanes of the Celts. St Columba was perhaps the most famous of these sea-borne travellers of early days, as he founded the community on the tiny island of Iona, from where Christianity was carried into northern Scotland. South Argyll remained the seat of Scottish power until the ninth century when the Scottish king Kenneth MacAlpin conquered the Picts of the north and moved his capital to Perthshire. In medieval times and beyond, the mountainous interior allowed later tribal groupings or clans to thrive without much contact with any kind of Lowland authority in the east. These clan territories eventually came under the sway of the Lords of the Isles in the fourteenth and fifteenth centuries, whose power at its height threatened the authority of the Stewart monarchs of Scotland.

Argyll furnished the Jacobite rebellions of the eighteenth century with many supporters. With their ultimate failure (at Culloden Moor), the suppression

LOCH CRERAN AND BEINN SGULAIRD At 3058 ft (932 m), Beinn Sgulaird qualifies as a Munro – a Scottish mountain over 3000 ft (914 m) high. Here a shaft of low sunlight bathes its slopes in gold at the end of a crisp autumn day.

WEST LOCH TARBERT

BED & BREAKFAST in Argyll.

which followed in turn led government in the far-off Lowlands to turn its attention to the economic conditions of the area. The founding of a fishing station at Tobermory on the island of Mull was just one example of authority's efforts to 'modernise' the primitive Highland economy. Similarly, a road-building programme was carried out in the eighteenth century, following on from the early military roads, of which perhaps the most famous was the road built by General Wade over the Rest and Be Thankful. This hill pass at the head of Glen Croe, west of Loch Lomond, is still one of the most spectacular gateways into the area.

Until almost the end of the eighteenth century, the Highlands, and Argyll along with them, were seen as remote, possibly hostile and frequented by a race who spoke a different language from Lowland Scotland and England. Then, in the dawning of the age of Romanticism, the notion of tourism was born, and people started to come to Argyll for pleasure. The diaries of William and Dorothy Wordsworth, for example, relate how they entered Argyll over the Rest and Be Thankful, exploring as early as 1803.

With the awakening of interest in the Highlands of Scotland as a romantic and unspoilt area populated by 'noble savages', there arose the so-called 'cult of the picturesque' which still draws tourists to the area today. Early visitors were in the minds of the promoters of the Callander and Oban Railway, which reached the western seaboard by 1880, with the aim of turning this once-peaceful village clustered round a sheltered bay into a fishing and cargo port servicing the Hebrides.

Yet though rail travel brought the grandeur of Argyll nearer the Victorian excursionists, seaways still had their role to play. As the crow flies, parts of Argyll such as Cowal lay near the centres of population in the west of the central belt – the Clydeside conurbation. Not only Oban developed as a resort; other places including Dunoon in Cowal and Rothesay on the island of Bute also catered for the holiday trade. This went beyond the mass exodus of the Glasgow Fair – the two weeks in July when Glaswegians took their main summer holiday. The Argyll resorts and other little communities bordering the Firth of Clyde took their share of the wealth created by the Victorian entrepreneurs and businessmen in the form of grand mansions, and more modest though still substantial dwellings. These country retreats or seaside townhouses add much to the character of the built heritage of the area today.

The situation of Argyll, it has to be said, with lots of high rugged ground on the edge of the Atlantic in the face of the prevailing moist south-westerly winds, encompasses some of the wettest spots in all of Scotland. Inveraray, for example, recorded a thirty-year annual average (1951-1980) of 80 inches (2036 mm) of rain – almost twice that of the island of Tiree, out in the western sea, lying low so that the rain clouds pass over! In essence, statistics suggest that Argyll is mild and wet in comparison to places further east, and that there are wide local differences, depending on the local terrain. In general, the prevailing mildness and

IONA FROM ERRAID
Cradle of Scottish Christianity, the island of Iona lies across the Sound of Iona from the Ross of Mull. Dun I is the island's highest point at 332 ft (101 m).

7

OBAN AND THE ISLAND OF KERRERA
Just how Oban and its bay are protected by the island of Kerrera is well seen here from the air. Mull fills the horizon to the right.

Scotland – Castle Sween in Knapdale. Medieval sculptured grave slabs are another speciality, to be viewed at places such as Kilmartin, south of Oban. Early carved crosses, of which perhaps the most famous example is the Kildalton Cross on Islay, are also worth seeing. Later grand mansions and castles also abound and range from the picturesquely ruined, such as Kilchurn by Loch Awe, to the spectacularly ornate as in Mount Stuart on the island of Bute. There are also wildlife parks and museums, cruises and excursions on the water and many other tourist attractions. Among the quirkier is the only railway on a Scottish island – from Craignure ferry pier to Torosay castle on Mull – or a trip deep into a Scottish mountain via the access tunnel to the Cruachan Power Station turbine hall.

softness of the air, widely commented on by visitors, is one of the beguiling features of Argyll. The occasional rain shower is the price paid for the spectacle of vivid green wooded slopes and the beauty of mossy woods, let alone the variety of glorious gardens, another Argyll speciality.

As well as gardens, the castles and monuments of the area are wide-ranging and of great historical significance, which is to be expected in an area which has played an important role in the story of Scotland. They include the earliest surviving stone castle in

While getting around, the main point to remember is that the ferry network, as well as giving access to the Hebridean islands, mostly from Oban, can shorten journey times on the mainland; for example, the Portavadie to Tarbert in Kintyre connection, or the Gourock to Dunoon link across the Clyde estuary.

Cowal

The ancient rocks scoured by glaciers into deep glens, then subsequently invaded by sea, give Cowal its characteristic claw shape, seeming to reach out in a pincer movement to grasp the island of Bute below it. The steep slopes, in many places densely planted, as well as the copious rainfall, can make the area a little sombre in places, though there are some natural woodlands to enjoy, especially around Strachur and Glen Branter. The extensive plantings in the north of the area comprise the Argyll Forest Park. The earliest of its kind to be created anywhere in Britain, it dates from 1935. These Forestry Commission grounds extend to 60,000 acres (24,282 ha) north-west of Loch Long, and offer a wide variety of walks and signposted trails.

Approaching from the north, another characteristic is the high ground of a rugged peninsula, rising to 2479 ft (755.6 m), known as Argyll's Bowling Green, which lies between the sea lochs of Loch Goil and Loch Long. This name is probably linked to the original Gaelic name referring to cattle-droving: *Buaile na Greine* – sunny cattle-fold. The highest hills in the area also guard the northern approaches to Cowal. These are the so-called 'Arrochar Alps', lying to the north-west of the Rest and Be Thankful, their saw-toothed, spiky profile a dominating feature. Nearby, and actually under the magic 3000 ft (914 m) contour which qualifies it as a Munro, is The Cobbler, one of

LOCH LONG means the ship loch. The Vikings sailed their longships to the head of the loch then transported them overland to reach Loch Lomond.

9

DUNOON PIER looks back to the great days of the Clyde steamers, when the estuary was a playground for the population of Clydeside's industrial communities.

the quirkiest of Scotland's mountains, topping the soaring vivid green and rocky slopes of Glen Croe.

Further south, roads meet up with the fjord-like sea lochs and there are magnificent views, even from the roadside, especially around the Kyles of Bute, the stretch of water which separates Cowal from Bute. Everywhere there is this sense of the sea's incursions to the land and an endless seaweed-draped shoreline glimpsed through trees – most noticeable, say, on the road from Strachur to Tighnabruaich looking across Loch Fyne.

The area's more obvious signs of antiquity include the gaunt ruins of Carrick Castle, on the west side of Loch Goil, dating mainly from the fifteenth century, though it was thought to stand on an earlier Norse site. Formerly a Campbell stronghold, the castle was

burned in 1685. On the other side of Cowal, on the east shore of Loch Fyne, stands Castle Lachlan, guarding a little bay of the same name. A stronghold of the MacLachlans and mostly dating from the sixteenth century, the fortress was destroyed after the last Jacobite rebellion in 1746.

A special characteristic of the area is the number of outstanding viewpoints. The B836 round the head of Loch Striven is rewarding, while the A8003 above the Kyles of Bute, linking with Tighnabruaich, is simply outstanding. Built as recently as 1969, this road has opportunities to take in breathtaking panoramic views, for example, southwards down the Kyles of Bute and across the Clyde to Ayrshire. Another wild and lofty viewpoint can be found on the road running west to Otter Ferry on Loch Fyne. This east-west route, bisecting Cowal and running across the grain of the uplands, climbs steeply above the 1000 ft (305 m) contour with views westward across Knapdale on the north of the Kintyre peninsula to the island of Jura. After a short study of the map and on a clear day, it is possible to work out where the Corryvreckan whirlpool lies, using the distinct hump of the island of Scarba as a marker on the horizon, more than 20 miles (32 km) to the north-west.

A quick way to discover the area is to take the ferry to Dunoon across the Clyde from Gourock. Dunoon's first recorded villa (actually a mock castle) was under construction as early as 1822, setting the tone for the transformation of this small hamlet into the Clyde's pre-eminent resort – a position which it held until well into the twentieth century. Today, Dunoon is a pleasant place with a good range of shopping and a long breezy promenade in traditional style. The town has a noted jazz festival and famous Highland Games: the Cowal Highland Gathering boasts the largest annual assembly of pipers in Scotland, the so-called 'March of a Thousand Pipers'.

However, Dunoon does have a history which predates its resort development. There was a castle here as long ago as 1296, when it was occupied by King Edward of England. A fortress survived here until 1685, its name recalled in Castle Hill, above the pier, which has the remains of the castle on it. Below Castle Hill is the famous statue of Highland Mary, the mysterious Mary Campbell associated with Robert Burns. She was born on a nearby farm and died in 1786.

At a sandbank at the north end of the town, the name Lazaretto Point recalls a quarantine station which was sited here during the Napoleonic Wars. A stone wall and turret survive to mark the station boundaries. Another curious name association is the Holy Loch, traditionally explained as being the site of a shipwreck of a vessel carrying a cargo of earth from

the Holy Land which was intended for the foundations of Glasgow Cathedral.

One of the chief glories of Cowal is the Younger Botanic Garden at Benmore, just a few miles from Dunoon. An important outstation of the Royal Botanic Garden in Edinburgh, the garden takes in 120 acres (48.5 ha) of the former estate of Benmore. There are over 200 different varieties of conifers, and 250 species of rhododendron. Its well-signposted trails include a longer hike to the magnificent viewpoint on Benmore Hill.

LOCH RIDDON AND THE KYLES OF BUTE
The island of Bute, separated from Cowal by only the narrow Kyles of Bute, is renowned for some of the best in Argyll scenery.

Bute

SCALPSIE BAY, BUTE, lies on the Highland Boundary Fault, geologically marking the edge of the Highlands. Softer Lowland scenery lies to the south.

All but moored to Cowal by the very short ferry crossing of the Kyles of Bute from Colintraive in Cowal, the attractive island of Bute is also reached by ferry from Wemyss Bay, itself within easy reach of Glasgow. The approach across the Firth of Clyde gives a good first impression of this popular holiday island on the Clyde.

The island straddles the Highland Boundary Fault. Northwards there are moorlands and scattered woods, while to the south, the more fertile lowland sandstone soils support good farmland and woods. Midway on the island, the curve of Rothesay Bay is ringed by sturdy properties, including many handsome villas and hotels of the Victorian and Edwardian eras. With its promenade and holiday cafes, Rothesay still carries the air of a traditional holiday resort, though the great days of the Clyde steamers and the annual exodus of the Glasgow Fair have long gone. Many leisure activities such as golf, fishing, bowling, sea angling, walking and sailing are still readily available on the island.

12

Bute Museum is one place where the sense is strongly conveyed of Rothesay formerly being a mecca for the teeming millions of Clydeside, effectively portraying the changes which the town has seen as holiday habits have altered. The first steamboats were calling as early as 1816 and by the 1820s the expanding town was building a reputation as a resort, outstripping its rival Dunoon. This resort development eclipsed its previous importance as a cotton town – the first cotton mill in Scotland was sited here, though transport problems, inevitable on an island, hampered the industry's development.

Opposite the museum, the setting is dominated by the curtain walls of ruined Rothesay Castle. It is slightly unexpected to find the substantial remains of a medieval castle right in the middle of the town, in a site of no immediately obvious defensive advantages, only minutes from the waterfront. This impressive fortress dates from the early thirteenth century, certainly in time to be stormed and captured by the Norseman in 1230. The original castle plan was for a circular wall of enclosure, with four drum towers added later. One survives today from the late thirteenth century.

Later still is the stout gatehouse, dating from the time of King James IV, towards the end of the fifteenth century. The castle was also frequented by the Stewart kings of the fourteenth century. King Robert III's son David became Duke of Rothesay in 1398 and the dukedom has been kept as the Scottish title for the sovereign's eldest son ever since, hence Prince Charles is the present Duke of Rothesay.

Rothesay can give a misleading impression of the rest of the island, which is very relaxed and peaceful. Unlike Arran with its tough granite mountains dominating the south-western horizon, Bute has no high ground, but instead a gentle, rolling landscape, sheltered and hidden. For generations of visitors to Bute, the island's beaches have been an attraction,

ROTHESAY CASTLE
The great curtain walls of Rothesay Castle enclose a circular courtyard, a feature unique in Scotland. This stronghold has been unoccupied for three centuries.

ST BLANE'S
CHAPEL, BUTE
*The glade
around the ruins
of twelfth-century
St Blane's Chapel
sheltered a religious
foundation dating
from the sixth century.
Remains of monks'
cells are still visible.*

Irish monastic colleges. The chapel named after Blane has been dated to around the late twelfth century. It sits in a sheltered bowl, a rocky hollow watched over by ancient trees and the site of Blane's original religious community. The ruined chapel, the most conspicuous feature on the site with its little graveyard, has a typical Norman rounded arch with zig-zag designs and diagonal patterns around the nave.

Though it is hard to imagine the location as it would have been when the monks tilled the soil of the fields below and the settlement was an important religious centre, an atmosphere of peaceful watchfulness is all but palpable.

especially on the west side with their views across to the island of Arran. The wide sweep of Ettrick Bay is understandably popular, while, to the south, Scalpsie Bay with its reddish-tinged sand sits right on the Highland Line. Furthest south, Kilchattan Bay has all the air of a tiny resort looking out to wide sandy reaches at low tide.

One particularly rewarding spot lies at the south of the island. There are no developments or facilities here and barely a car park, but St Blane's Chapel is worth visiting simply for its sense of tranquillity. St Blane was born in Bute in the sixth century, a nephew of Cattan who was a fellow student with Columba in one of the

From the chapel, an ancient track formerly used by worshippers goes over Suidhe Hill to the north and down to Kilchattan Bay – a reminder of the choice of walks and trails which the island offers.

Scotland is noted for its castles and stately homes, from ruined fragments to grand mansions. However, no other stately pile is quite like Mount Stuart, seat of the Marquesses of Bute.

The visitors of old who thronged to Bute in former days enjoyed the promenade and the cruises, the beaches and the walks. They watched the steamers ply the Clyde's waters from the high point of Canada Hill behind the town, or admired the pot plants and gaudy bedding displays in The Esplanade Gardens. But only in recent years has Mount Stuart House and Gardens been opened up so that today's tourist can see its idiosyncratic splendour.

The present Mount Stuart owes much to the Third Marquess of Bute, described as the richest man in Britain at his coming-of-age in 1868. He was also a scholar, historian, archaeologist, mystic and patron of the arts. The first Mount Stuart was gutted by fire in 1877, creating the opportunity for him to express his artistic aspirations, his love of romanticism and his complex personality in the Mount Stuart seen today.

He commissioned Sir Robert Rowand Anderson to design it – which is perhaps why the grand Gothic statement which resulted has more than a passing resemblance to the National Portrait Gallery in Edinburgh, another of Anderson's creations.

At the heart of Mount Stuart is the Marble Hall, a vast room with marble pillars and soaring arches pointing upwards to a Gothic arcade and high-level stained glass with the signs of the zodiac, topped by shimmering stars. Tapestries line the walls and off this echoing space are the principal rooms, such as the panelled dining room with its important portraits including work by Raeburn and Ramsay. Other highlights include the Drawing Room with its religious paintings and heraldic decorations.

The whole effect of the house is unlike any other stately home north of the border. Out of doors, the grounds, or more correctly in Scots, the policies, are likewise built on an ambitious scale, with long vistas disappearing into distant green shade.

MOUNT STUART
One of Scotland's most distinctive and characterful stately homes, everything about Mount Stuart on the Isle of Bute is built on a grand scale.

Around Loch Fyne

INVERARAY
One of the most
attractive townscapes
anywhere in Scotland,
Inveraray owes its
appearance to the plan
of the Third Duke
of Argyll.

Loch Fyne is a classic Scottish fjord. Part of a western seaboard river system which followed the grain and folding of the ancient rocks before the Ice Ages, the riverbed was scoured deep by glacier action then drowned by the sea. Loch Fyne in more recent times had an important herring fishery. The little settlements along its coast had their origins as fishing communities, though the nineteenth-century boom has long gone, leaving the cottages as holiday homes for the folk from Glasgow and beyond. As early as 1805, it was reported that at least 500 large herring boats were on the loch. The fishery here had originally been hampered by lack of communication with Glasgow, the main market. There were difficulties getting in barrels and salt for processing. It was to facilitate this trade that the roads from the south bank of Loch Fyne through Cowal were originally built in the early nineteenth century.

However, Loch Fyne had more than fishing. Like Bonawe on Loch Etive, it had a thriving smelting industry, which was set up in 1754. As in other western locations most of the ore was imported, while some say most of the woodlands were devastated. Other historians argue that the ironmasters coppiced the western woods, as it was in their interests to maintain a supply of the poles which spring from a cut stump, as these made good charcoal. They suggest that it was indiscriminate grazing which finished off so much native woodland. Whatever the truth of the matter, the old smelting industry is recalled by the village of Furnace on the shores of the loch.

Though the most impressive approach to Inveraray

is from the north-east, down the A83 from the head of Loch Fyne, no matter the direction, an impression is given of a harmonious little town, architecturally speaking, with a wealth of Georgian detailing in its buildings. It was, in fact, designed all of a piece by Archibald, Third Duke of Argyll, after he took the title in 1743. He planned a new castle and a new town (a discreet distance away, naturally). Inveraray is one of the few Scottish towns re-modelled by the great improving landowners of the eighteenth century as a result of aesthetic considerations alone. He consulted with the architect Roger Morris, while the even better-known John Adam was also involved.

The façade of the waterfront buildings, as seen from the north, is particularly pleasing. Also notable from the north is the series of handsome bridges which bring the road into town. John Adam, Roger Morris and the later Robert Mylne were involved in their design. The waterfront buildings include the Town House and a hotel which was originally intended for the use of visiting judges, lawyers and other officials, as Inveraray was the seat of an important court. The original courthouse and prison also stood on the waterfront but were replaced by later buildings. They in turn are now occupied by the visitor attraction Inveraray Jail, which brings alive the conditions in a nineteenth-century prison by way of an authentically dressed warder and prisoner, as well as lifelike tableaux, which capture the workings of an 1820 courtroom.

Aside from exploring the town, with its array of small shops and elegant buildings, many visitors also take in Inveraray Castle, the home of the present Duke of Argyll, sometimes known as MacCaillean More,

Chief of the Clan Campbell. They first came over the hills to Inveraray in the fifteenth century. Previously, their power-base had been Innischonnell Castle on one of the little islands on Loch Awe, above Portinsherrich. Eventually, protected by their fortress, a scattering of houses – old Inveraray – ran down towards the shore.

The Third Duke of Argyll decided to replace the old fortress with something much more grand. Though building began as early as 1744, the plan was only completed in 1788 by the Fifth Duke. By this time a new town had sprung up as well, with the old one cleared away from the castle grounds. The conical turrets which give it a château-like air today were added after the castle suffered a fire in 1877. Within the castle, many treasures are

INVERARAY CASTLE is the seat of the Dukes of Argyll, chiefs of the Clan Campbell.

LOCH FYNE
Looking west from its
northern headlands
towards the Arrochar
Alps. So indented is
the Argyll coastline
that from this point it
is almost forty miles
(64 km) by water
to the mouth of
Loch Fyne.

may be a peaceful little spot today but during World War II it played an important role as a secret training base, particularly for the development of sea-borne assault landing techniques put into practice in many major commando raids, culminating in D-day itself. Photographs, contemporary documents and scale models create a fascinating display. Inveraray also has a famous bell tower. This 126 ft (38.4 m) granite tower features the world's second heaviest ring of ten bells. There is an exhibition and it is possible to climb to the top of the tower via an easy staircase.

Not far from the town round the head of the loch by the A83 is the Ardkinglas Woodland Garden at Cairndow. Here there is a fine conifer collection, including at least twenty trees over 120 ft (36.5 m) high and a silver fir with a girth of 30 ft (9 m). Best time to visit is late spring and early summer when the rhododendrons and other shrubs are in bloom.

displayed. There is a state dining room, complete with gold plates for formal occasions. Magnificent Beauvais tapestries adorn the Tapestry Room, while the huge Armoury Hall has a ceiling almost 100 ft (30.5 m) above the floor and is filled with historic weaponry, including the muskets issued to the Argyll Militia who fought on the government side at Culloden.

Inveraray has even more to offer. Making the façade of the town even more like the backdrop for some period drama are the masts of an old-fashioned vessel tied up to the quay. This is the *Arctic Penguin*, a former lightship. Built in 1911 and a very rare example of a riveted iron vessel, she now houses an exhibition on the maritime heritage of the western seaboard. Also within easy reach of the town, in the grounds of Inveraray Castle, is the Combined Operations Museum. Inveraray

Between Furnace and Inveraray lies one of the most fascinating rural places in all of Argyll, the former farm-village of Auchindrain. From the Gaelic *achadh nan droighinn*, meaning field of blackthorn, Auchindrain was, more accurately, a multiple tenancy farming community – a surviving example of a kind of farming widespread in Scotland in earlier days but now practically vanished. By the early 1960s, Auchindrain had become the first open-air museum in Scotland and almost the only one in Britain based on a set of buildings formerly occupied but kept in museum form on their original sites.

These buildings – 20 in all – range in origin from the eighteenth to the twentieth century, evolving and being reworked as farming practice demanded. The

site now has a building that the last tenant farmers could never have imagined – a display centre and shop where the background of the unique site is explained. Afterwards, the visitor can stroll round, peeping into the buildings, with their box beds and attached byres, their tools and implements, outlandish to modern eyes. A whole half-lost vocabulary emerges: crusie for the primitive rush lights which lit the dwellings; kailyard, where hardy vegetables of the cabbage type were grown; stook, a wedge of sheaves set up to dry; trevis, the partition between cattle in the byre… and so on. There are examples of the typically northern Scottish longhouse, which as its name suggests is

basically living accommodation and a byre in a long line – which at least meant the farmer did not have to go out on a dark wet night to check his cattle.

More than a glimpse can also be gained of the everyday life. As on all small holdings the stock had to be attended to, fodder laid in, and cultivating, sowing and reaping carried out in their due season. Peat supplied the heat, willow the baskets and creels; straw, rushes or bracken became both roofing material and animal bedding. With enough manpower on site, larger tasks such as the reaping of fields became a social occasion – all was not misery and toil – certainly not with game on the hill and Loch Fyne herring close by.

LOCH FYNE FROM THE AIR
Glaciers dispersing from the south-west Grampians cut the ribbon-like lochs of Argyll. Subsequent dipping of the land allowed the sea to invade, most spectacularly in the case of Loch Fyne.

19

LOCH GAIR
Though only an inlet in the long miles of shoreline along Loch Fyne, Loch Gair provides an anchorage for today's pleasure craft – a reminder of the attraction of these sheltered waters for sailing enthusiasts.

It is simply not possible to travel very far in Argyll without encountering a special garden. The main A83 down Loch Fyne is no exception and goes past one of the finest in Scotland. Crarae Garden is an outstanding woodland garden. Copious rains, acid soils, and no extremes of winter temperatures around sea level provide the conditions for spectacular plantings. Crarae is built along the steep wooded sides of Crarae Glen. Many horticulturalists enthuse about the special ambience which lingers here, likening it to some wild Himalayan foothill.

A burn runs in the glen, falling to Loch Fyne, and it is this wild water which gives the garden much of its charm. The garden was started first of all near Crarae House in 1912 by Lady Campbell, with some shrub and eucalyptus plantings. Her son extended the forestry theme with yews and Chinese firs. The shallow soil and the humidity were ideal for rhodo-

dendrons, growing in the dappled shade of a natural woodland. The rhododendron family's long flowering season, from February through to July, ensures colour right through the first part of the year. Other species of trees and shrubs provide a balance, as do the smaller-scale primulas and poppies, and the early spring bulbs. The overall effect is of restraint and harmony. Nevertheless Crarae offers an exciting display appreciated by even the most casual of gardeners.

Further down the A83, round the headland where the road turns into Loch Gilp, is another garden. The plantings at Kilmory Castle started as far back as the 1770s and are gradually being restored. Kilmory Castle is very close to Lochgilphead, a neat little town, with white-painted frontages along its main street. It is very much a junction-town or route centre, servicing Knapdale and mid Argyll.

Kintyre

The fjord of West Loch Tarbert marks the northern boundary of the peninsula of Kintyre, from where it is all but 40 miles (64 km) to the southern tip at the Mull of Kintyre. In general, the relief here is lower than in many of the more rugged parts of the western seaboard, though much of the interior of Kintyre is moderately high moorland, forested in places. Kintyre stands in the same latitude as Ayrshire and at least in its lower end has a distinctly 'un-Highland' feel. Indeed, its history of plantations by the Campbells of Argyll, who were of Lowland stock, and its agricultural leaning towards dairy farming – another Ayrshire parallel – suggest that it is set apart from Highland Argyll. Besides, the lack of really high ground does not draw cloud, so that the rainfall is lighter than in many other parts of the western seaboard.

Yet the farms and fields of the west and south, particularly noticeable on the coastal flats and the raised beaches by the main road, are not truly Lowland. The sea views from the A83 to Campbeltown are dominated by the westward profiles of the islands of Islay and rugged Jura, set across a sparkling sea as the sun goes down. Kintyre, in essence, is a mix of both Highland and Lowland, with the wild moorlands

at the Mull of Kintyre a reminder of the rugged nature of Argyll, and the wild empty reach of the sands at Machrihanish strongly reminiscent of the surf-swept beaches of the Hebrides.

Tarbert is the northern gateway to Kintyre and is an attractive little place gathered round East Loch Tarbert, with West Loch Tarbert barely a mile away, all but making Kintyre an island. As in other Scottish Tarberts (or Tarbets) the name literally means 'boat-drag' or place where boats were manhandled from one stretch of water to another. Most famously, this was undertaken by Magnus Barefoot, a Norse king who dragged his vessels across the isthmus in 1093. This

TARBERT

is still a commercial fishing port. Inevitably, from earliest days, the narrow isthmus and gateway to Kintyre has been a stronghold. Tarbert Castle, above the harbour, was once occupied by Robert the Bruce.

good range of shops, set around the sea inlet of Campbeltown Loch. It formerly had an important herring fishery, as well as 30 distilleries in the town (now there are two). It even had a coal mine nearby, which closed in 1967. Now Campbeltown is noted for its creamery, using the produce from the dairy herds in the area. In 1997, a ferry service was started between Campbeltown and Ballycastle, Co. Antrim, which, it is hoped, will bring benefits to the local economy.

Campbeltown owes its origins to Archibald Campbell, Seventh Earl of

SKIPNESS POST OFFICE & SHOP
Skipness lies in a pleasant corner of Kintyre. The village post office and shop are an important, and attractive, part of the local community.

story is touched upon at An Tairbeart Heritage Centre, just south of Tarbert, and much else besides of Tarbert's heritage, including wildlife, natural resources and the local history of the area. There is also a children's play area, farm animals and frequent craft demonstrations.

Apart from Tarbert, Campbeltown is the only town of any size in Kintyre, a full 138 miles (222 km) by main road from Glasgow, yet only about 65 miles (104 km) as the crow flies. Fortunately it also has a direct air connection. It is a work-a-day town, with a

Argyll, who built a castle on a little hill above the natural harbour in the early seventeenth century. He encouraged Lowlanders to settle, thereby both stimulating trade and developing agriculture, so that by 1700 the town had been granted status as a royal burgh. A burgh in Scotland was formerly a town with trading rights and the right to hold fairs and markets. If granted by the king, the town was a royal burgh. By the late eighteenth century it could boast some fine civic buildings, including a notable town house (c 1760) replacing an earlier tolbooth. By the mid

nineteenth century, Campbeltown was involved in fishing, boat-building and distilling as well as processing flax.

All burghs marked the centre of the town, meeting place and site of fairs, with a mercat (market) cross. The thrifty citizens of Campbeltown 'borrowed' a magnificent fourteenth-century disc-headed carved Christian cross as their mercat cross, moving it from Kilkivan some time in the seventeenth century and setting it up in their new town. It can still be seen today, in the middle of a roundabout, complete with figurative scenes (look for the mermaid and the sea monster) and interlaced decorative work.

Of the two peripheral routes round Kintyre which go to Campbeltown, the east-coast route is the slower, crossing the mouths of the little green glens running down from the interior, by way of forests and rocky headlands, all the while with views to Arran across Kilbrannan Sound. The west coast road is faster, often running below stranded cliffs, with raised beaches between road and sea.

Rich in early sites, Kintyre has a wealth of ancient places such as standing stones, vitrified forts, cup and ring marked stones and other such features difficult to interpret. A little later, St Columba had a presence here. A strong tradition – perhaps even a historical fact – relates how he first landed on Scottish soil at the foot of the peninsula, just west of Southend, on his way to Iona in AD 563. The site is recalled in the nearby ancient chapel of Kilcolmkil (Columba's chapel), dating from the thirteenth century, complete with ancient gravestones and, intriguingly, on the top of an adjoining small knoll, the imprint of two right feet carved into the bedrock. These are known as Columba's footsteps, though it is suggested that one of them predates Columba by at least a thousand years.

KINTYRE
The east coast of Kintyre stretches northwards from Campbeltown Loch, with the minor road by its shores giving grand views east across Kilbrannan Sound to Arran. This road runs for almost thirty twisting miles (48 km) to Claonaig, where there is a summer ferry connection with Arran.

along with some sculptured carved tombstones. These represent some of the finest medieval graveslabs in Argyll, with motifs including hounds, stags, galleys and armed warriors.

The carving of ornate graveslabs in medieval times has been classified into various schools by archaeologists – and the Kintyre school has its own style seen, for example, in the graveslabs at the Old Parish Church at Killean by the main road to Campbeltown.

CAMPBELTOWN, near the end of the long Kintyre peninsula, is a busy town with direct air connections to Glasgow and a ferry service to Northern Ireland.

MULL OF KINTYRE, (opposite), the southernmost tip of Kintyre, seen here from Keil Point to the east at dusk.

Sites with carved footprints are thought to relate to an early ritual associated with kingship or some kind of chief's ceremony. The Columba story was added later.

About five hundred years after Columba, there occurs a character associated strongly with this area: Somerled (d 1164), who rallied the native people against the marauding Norsemen and became the progenitor of the Clan Donald, the Lords of the Isles. Either he or his son Reginald built Saddell Abbey, midway down the east side of the peninsula. At one time, after Iona, no ecclesiastical seat in the west was held in higher regard. Saddell Abbey took the form of a cross, precisely orientated to the main compass points and set in a peaceful wooded valley. Yet only the ruined gables of this well-wrought twelfth-century religious foundation of the Cistercians stand today,

Another notable historic site, at the top of the peninsula overlooking the sea, is Skipness Castle. It started as a hall-house and separate chapel in the thirteenth century, subsequently incorporated by curtain walls in the early fourteenth century to form a courtyard. The fortress was held for the Macdonald chiefs until the end of the time of the Lords of the Isles in 1493. The chapel was dedicated to St Brendan.

Finally, all touring visitors, while making their way south by the fast A83 for the first time, probably wonder if it is worth going all the way to the Mull of Kintyre, famed in song. It is an extra 15 miles (24 km) by road down to the lighthouse beyond Campbeltown. Best to go in the evening, to view the sunset and look across to Ireland, barely 14 miles (22.5 km) away to the south-west.

Gigha

Barely 6 miles (9.6 km) long, Gigha lies close to the Kintyre peninsula, and was once an important anchorage or place of shelter on the sea-route down Kintyre. The Caolas Gigalum near the south tip of the island even sheltered the longships of King Haakon of Norway's fleet in 1263, before their defeat at the Battle of Largs.

The first impression of Gigha is that it is more lush and fertile than many Hebridean islands, with a good proportion of arable land as well as woodland. The main centre for the island is the scattered village of Ardminish, with the only general store and post office. There is also a friendly hotel. To the south are the ruins of the thirteenth-century St Catan's Chapel (Kilchattan). Nearby is an ogam stone, showing good examples of this curious ancient Celtic form of writing. There are other standing stones on the island.

With thousands of years of continuous settlements, according to archaeological finds, small wonder that Gigha is rich in folklore. At Beathag's Well (*Tobar a' Bheathaig* in Gaelic) by East Tarbert Bay, a local tradition says that a fair wind will be granted to sailors who throw a little of the well water in the required direction and leave a small payment nearby. Meanwhile, a small lochan, Tarr an Tairbh, is said to be inhabited by a water-bull, close cousin to the water-horse of Gaelic tradition, though this shy beast is seen only by locals.

Gigha has caves to explore and fine sandy beaches, including one in the north of the island off which the royal yacht *Britannia* has anchored, as the sands are a

favourite picnic place of the royal family.

One of the best-known gardens in Argyll is on Gigha. Achamore House Gardens were created in 1944 by Sir James Horlick on a 50-acre (20-ha) site. Massed daffodils near the house are a spring feature, while the Pond Garden is brightened by the lemon yellow spathes of skunk cabbage. In the Ash Garden, hostas with their glaucous leaves grow in profusion. The overall effect is that there are 'gardens within a garden'.

However, it is massed rhododendrons and azaleas which offer the finest effects and make this a garden to visit in late spring. Look for the path to the superb viewpoint which reveals Jura's hills rising out of the sea and, further round, the hills of Ireland.

OLD STONE HARBOUR at Ardminish Bay, Gigha, next to where the ferry comes in.

GIGHA, seen from Creag Bhan, its highest point (opposite). Gigha has a distinct personality all of its own, and with thousands of years of continuous occupation, the island is rich in folklore.

east, where it shares features with lonely Jura, its near neighbour, and the hard sparkle of quartz gives the hills a rugged look.

Islay was formerly a very important Hebridean island, acting as a kind of capital on the western seaboard in the days of the Lords of the Isles. It was originally part of the kingdom of Dalriada, settled by the Scots from Ireland, before coming under Norse rule for about three centuries from around AD 850. The island is associated with Clan Donald, whose progenitor, Somerled, defeated the Viking forces in a sea battle and made Islay the clan powerbase. Clan Donald are associated with Dunyvaig Castle which overlooks Lagavulin Bay in the south.

Islay and Jura

LOCH GRUINART These wild and empty tidal reaches attract birds and seals in plenty. Here many hundreds of barnacle geese roost in fading October light.

Islay is sometimes described as an exception in Hebridean terms. This is a reference to the fact that thanks mainly to geology there is much good agricultural land. There are bands of limestone and also a fertile mix of boulder clay and windblown sand. This in turn means that there are substantial farms rather than marginal crofts, particularly notable in the area around Bowmore and Loch Gruinart, for example.

There is a wildness to Islay as well, especially in the

However, the most significant site associated with the Macdonalds lies towards the north end of the island at Loch Finlaggan, close to the main road to the Jura ferry. Two islands close together on the loch are, according to recent research, the place where Clan Donald, who became the Lords of the Isles, held their clan parliaments. Dozens of buildings, including domestic dwellings, a chapel and a chief's hall, have been identified only by their foundations, as little can be seen above ground. The story is told in an interpretation centre nearby.

There are substantial quantities of peat on Islay, linked to the island's other industry – whisky distilling, which provides employment for the local population. Any whisky connoisseur will find a journey round Islay quite familiar territory, with names like Bowmore, Bruichladdich, Lagavulin, Port Ellen, Ardbeg, Bunnahabhain, Caol Ila and Laphroaig, cropping up on signposts as well as providing a variety of challenges in pronunciation at the bar counter. About four million gallons of whisky leave the island every year. Add to this the magnificent beaches and seascapes, a wealth of early historic sites and a variety of habitat that has made Islay a magnet for birdwatchers, and the result is an island with a very distinct personality and decidedly different ambience from the rest of the Hebrides.

On the topic of birds, just one of the specialities is the chough. It is recognised by a bright red bill and legs and a high wheezy call. In winter, Islay plays host to – some estimate – up to one-sixth of the entire world population of barnacle geese, especially around the open reaches by Laggan Bay.

The settlement on Islay reflects the economic factors at work here. The typical Hebridean crofting township is more or less absent; instead the settlement is in clusters, villages or small towns which service activities such as dairy processing or distilling. Bowmore is typical of the settlements on Islay. It gives its name to the whisky made in the distillery hard by the sea edge at the foot of the town. It was originally laid out in 1768 by the local landowner, Daniel

Campbell of Shawfield, following the usual desire to remove settlement from the sight of large residences, in this case, Islay House by the head of Loch Indaal. The new village was built around the main street which runs from the pierhead to the church. At Port Charlotte, above the road in a converted kirk, is the Museum of Islay Life. The ferry from the mainland arrives at another of Islay's villages, Port Ellen, founded in the 1820s by the laird, Walter Campbell, who named it after his wife.

There are many wild seascapes in the west of the island. It is worth exploring Machir Bay, for example, with its superb beaches, practically deserted for much of the year. Inland is the ruined kirk of Kilchoman. There are some impressive graveslabs in the kirkyard, as well as two crosses of late medieval date, from the

LOCH FINLAGGAN & CHAPEL
The islands on Loch Finlaggan contain important ruins belonging to Clan Donald, who became the Lords of the Isles. According to recent research, this former power base is where they held their clan parliaments.

THE PAPS OF JURA
From across the Sound of Islay, the Paps of Jura with their steep angles and shimmering quartzite slopes are amongst the most distinctive of Scottish peaks.

Iona school of carving. North of Machrie, at Saligo, in rough weather it is easy to believe that the breakers have rolled all the way from America. A little way east on the road up the west side of Loch Gruinart to Kilnave there are fine views over the sandy wastes of the tidal loch. There is a ruined chapel here associated with the aftermath of a nearby clash between the Macleans and the Macdonalds in 1598. This followed the granting of land on Islay to the Macleans from Mull by King James VI. The Macdonalds objected to this arrangement, and when an army of around 400 Macleans came to make their claim, they were met with fierce resistance from the already resident Macdonalds. About 30 Macleans, fleeing from the fight, sought refuge in the chapel. Refusing to acknowledge this place of sanctuary, the Macdonalds

set its roof alight and the fugitives died within it. A weathered eighth-century carved cross can also be seen in the kirkyard.

At the southern end of the island, down beyond the sweeping curve of the sands of Laggan Bay, the promontory of the Oa juts out, with caves and cliffs to explore. The memorial on the Mull of Oa, at the tip, recalls the sinking of the troopships *Tuscania*, by torpedo, and *Otranto*, wrecked, in 1918, when 650 men lost their lives. The memorial is the work of the American Red Cross.

The southern end of Islay is the home of what is sometimes described as the finest carved cross in Scotland. The eighth/ninth-century Kildalton Cross was carved from a slab of epidorite, a grey rock from which has been fashioned a ring cross with elaborate work in the style of the Iona school.

The island of Jura offers a huge contrast with Islay. It could hardly be otherwise in a rugged landscape with one road, one distillery, six sporting estates and around 5000 red deer, outnumbering the human population by around twenty to one. For the keen-eyed, there are little hints and clues of a previous life on Jura, before the island, like so much of the Highlands, was cleared of its original settlements. Former places of occupation are often marked by the faint remains of 'lazy-beds', the strip cultivation practised in the far west, just apparent today as parallel stripes on the moor and pasture.

From the ferry pier, the main road climbs away from the coast, passing Am Fraoch Eilean (Gaelic: heather island) in the Sound of Islay. On the island are the remains of a twelfth-century tower house built by

Somerled, founder of the Clan Donald, to control the Sound. Further on, past Jura House with its exotic gardens, the road gives fine views west across empty moorland to the Paps of Jura, with their streams of glittering grey quartz screes. The pale quartz breaks down to poor soil, hence the extensive peat bog of the interior. Explorers staying on the road get no more than a hint of the truly empty quarter which lies to the west. Back on the east side, the road peters out – as far as its suitability for ordinary saloon cars. The more determined explorers can make their way north on foot (or on high clearance vehicles), past the house of Barnhill in which George Orwell wrote *Nineteen Eighty-four*. Some come this way en route for the wild waters of the whirlpool of the Corryvreckan, the most famous whirlpool or tide race in Scotland, at its most spectacular when a west wind runs against a west-running flood tide.

All of Jura's 200 inhabitants stay on the east coast, many around the only place which can be described as a population centre, Craighouse, also the location of the distillery which takes its name from the place.

JURA FROM THE AIR
A flavour of the wild and trackless nature of Jura can be gained here looking south from the northern end of the island to the distant Paps.

31

Colonsay

Colonsay is barely 8 miles (13 km) long. Beyond its western shores lies Canada, give or take a couple of lighthouses. Some visitors take their cars, as there are at least 14 miles (22.5 km) of public road. The limy sandstone breaks down to form good soil, hence Colonsay's farms raise sheep and cattle. The machair is shadowed by hunting buzzards, while wild goats browse round the edges of protected patches of unusual Hebridean natural woodlands of oak, hazel and willow – broadleaved species dwarfed by exposure to form miniature thickets tucked into the rolling brackeny moors. The habitat list also includes gleaming sandy beaches and extensive tidal sandflats as well as impressive sea cliffs.

One of the finest beaches is at Kiloran Bay towards the north end of the island. In 1882, a ninth-century Viking warrior burial was discovered in the dunes behind the bay, complete with ship, as well as weapons and coins. Colonsay is also of interest to visitors with an appreciation of early history. There are duns (early

32

hill forts), burial cairns, standing stones and other prehistoric paraphernalia scattered over the island.

On the rough grazing behind Kiloran Bay, it is often possible to see choughs, another island speciality, as on Mull. These are just one of the 150 species on the island's bird-list. Botanists, too, visit to check out the 500 recorded plant species found here – one of the most extensive lists of all the Hebridean islands.

The island once belonged to the Macphees, who were the scribes and recorders for the deeds of the Lords of the Isles. Thereafter Colonsay was associated with Macdonalds, Campbells and MacNeils. The benevolent approach of the last-named family meant that the island escaped the worst ravages of the Clearances, though voluntary emigration tempted many to the New World, in common with many other Highland communities of the nineteenth century. Of the hundred or so inhabitants today, perhaps a fifth still speak Gaelic and several families go back many generations on the island – again unlike many parts of the west. The island was bought by Lord Strathcona in 1905 and remains in the hands of his descendants. The present Lord Strathcona lives at Kiloran House, originally built by the MacNeils in 1722. Surrounded by woods in a sheltered valley, many interesting and exotic plant species thrive in the mild air of Kiloran Gardens.

South of Colonsay is the much smaller island of Oronsay, separated from Colonsay at low water only by a mile of sandflats, called the Strand, a splashy cockle-strewn haunt of wading birds (and visitors glancing anxiously at their watches, wondering if they could have misread the tide timetables).

The crossing is worth making to see Oronsay

Priory. This abandoned Augustinian House was founded in the second quarter of the fourteenth century by John, Lord of the Isles. It probably covers the original site of the monastery founded by St Oran in AD 563. St Oran was a companion of St Columba (Colonsay is Columba's island in Old Norse). The surviving complex shows a series of building phases between the fourteenth and sixteenth centuries, with graveslabs and sombre grey warriors carved on top. Nearby is a magnificent early sixteenth-century cross, commemorating Prior Colin who died in 1510. Offshore the complex series of reefs and skerries surrounding Eilean na Ron (Gaelic: seal island) are an important breeding area for grey seals. Roaring bull seals can be heard in the autumn, when wind and tide are still.

ORONSAY CROSS

The religious complex at Oronsay Priory was second only to Iona in importance. The impressive 12 ft (3.7 m) high Celtic cross is even visible from the north end of Loch Gruinart on Islay.

ISLE OF JURA FROM ABOVE TAYVALLICH *Like so many places in the Highlands, Jura was cleared of many of its original settlements.*

Knapdale to Oban

Knapdale is the name given to the part of Argyll lying between the Crinan Canal in the north and West Loch Tarbert in the south. The main road hugs the east coast, while the western seaboard is spectacularly indented. Car travellers should bear in mind that neither road running by Loch Sween allows a loop to be made and that a return journey almost back to Crinan is necessary. However, the B8024 does offer a circular route via the southern shore of Loch Caolisport.

In Knapdale, the grain of the land, running north-east to south-west and caused by complex folding of ancient rocks, is conspicuous. This is made even more notable because the troughs in the folds have been deepened by glaciers and then, in the case of Loch Sween and Loch Caolisport, invaded by the sea. The overwhelming impression is of the softness of the climate and woodlands. Honeysuckle runs rampant over mossy walls and deep green tree-trunks. Though the poor soils work against farming, the extensive forestry plantings have supplemented the native woodlands. Especially notable in any exploration of Knapdale are the surviving native oakwoods, notably around Loch Sween where the luxuriance of the tree cover is a reminder of the mild climate.

Scientists believe that these oakwoods with their rare ferns, lichens and mosses are actually older than the Caledonian pine forests of the east, as the mild Atlantic waters kept the coastal fringes ice-free during the Ice Ages. Thus they represent a strand of Scotland's story running back for perhaps millions of years.

Historic themes which occur in Kintyre are also encountered in Knapdale. There are fine collections of West Highland grave slabs to view, this time of the Loch Sween school of carving, for example, at Kilberry off the B8024 on the west side of Knapdale.

Also of note is the thirteenth-century chapel at Keills, 5 miles (8 km) beyond Tayvallich by the west shore of Loch Sween. There are fine medieval tombstones by the chapel, while uphill from the site stands the Keills Cross, probably tenth century. Its central boss is a bird's nest whose three eggs symbolise the Holy Trinity. Weathering of the cross has all but removed the carving of a hooded figure with an Irish type of pastoral staff. Keills as a place name suggests a Celtic monastic community.

Between Loch Sween and Loch Caolisport at Kilmory Knap, another thirteenth-century chapel has notable grave monuments from medieval times, while

KEILLS CROSS
The art of the West Highland schools of stone carvers produced masterpieces like the tenth-century Keills Cross, now located in a chapel at Keillmore, opposite Jura.

35

CASTLE SWEEN
Probably the most significant ancient monument in Knapdale, the castle sits on a rocky shoulder above Loch Sween. It is described as the oldest castle on the Scottish mainland and in spite of its early date, the main walls remain in a good state of preservation.

sometimes described as the oldest surviving stone castle on mainland Scotland. It sits on a rocky shoulder above Loch Sween, adjacent to a caravan park. In spite of its early date its main walls remain in a state of good preservation. The walling was extensively overhauled by Historic Scotland in the 1980s.

Castle Sween was built around eight centuries ago by Suibhne, the progenitor of the Clan MacSween, and comprises a rectangular enclosure with substantial buttressing of the walls. The interior would have had timber buildings erected against the walls and these interior ranges can still be traced by way of the slots and recesses for supporting the internal accommodation. Towers were added later, probably in the fifteenth century.

Not a great deal is known about the castle's history, except that it is likely to have been besieged by Robert the Bruce in the Scots Wars of Independence. By this time the castle was within the sway of the Lords of the Isles. The MacNeills of Gigha became the keepers of the castle, though it later passed – almost inevitably, in this part of the west – to the all-powerful Campbells. It remained in their hands till 1645, when it was burned by royalist forces under Colkitto (*Coll Ciotach*, 'left-handed Coll'), Alasdair MacDonald. In spite of the austere castle exterior, the life of a powerful local leader in such a fortress would have been surprisingly sophisticated, given the rich treasury of the Gaelic oral and musical tradition and the later trading links with other parts of Europe.

Only 10 miles (16 km) to the north lies the boundary of Knapdale at the Crinan Canal. This was conceived as a means of avoiding the long sea passage

outside stands the fifteenth-century Cross of Alexander McMillan of Kilmory, with a hunting scene on one side and a Crucifixion and a sword on the other.

The north side of Loch Caolisport has a cave associated with St Columba, who, presumably, must have just dropped in while on his way to Iona via Southend, his first port of call. Whatever the truth, the cave is traditionally associated with his arrival in Scotland. It contains a rock-shelf with an altar and carved crosses. The site had much earlier Stone Age occupants. It is accessible on foot either from the Ellary or Kilmory road end.

However, probably the most significant ancient monument in Knapdale is Castle Sween. This is round the Mull of Kintyre, which at the time would have saved a sail of about two days. It was authorised by Parliament in 1793. The enterprising and improving Duke of Argyll was behind the scheme, seeing it as a kind of 'job-creation' scheme and also a way of enhancing the local economy, particularly with the developing fisheries out in the west, around the Hebrides.

Building the canal across the 9-mile (14.5-km) neck of land by way of the edge of the Crinan Moss proved no easy task; the unstable nature of the soft ground dictated that the canal was built hard against the steeply sloping ground to the south of the Moss.

Though opened in 1801, construction problems, and a shortage of funds, meant a continuing programme of works was carried out till 1809. Even then, the canal needed extensive repairs, so that by 1816 the redoubtable Scottish engineer Thomas Telford had been called in to oversee and suggest renovative works. Since that time, the canal has remained little altered, though the basins at both ends have been enlarged. Each time a vessel leaves the Loch

Crinan end, about a quarter of a million gallons of water goes out with it, so that the canal is fed by an ingenious system of reservoirs in the hills above.

Atmospheric and attractive, particularly at the Crinan end, the emphasis on canal usage has swung away from fishing craft (though it still has some inshore traffic) towards yachts and pleasure vessels which, again, all add to the colour and cheerful atmosphere of Crinan.

Passing on northwards beyond Knapdale and over

DUNADD FORT FROM THE AIR
Dunadd Fort on its hilltop dominates Crinan Moss. It was once the home of the kings of the Scots of Dalriada in the sixth century.

and, most significantly, a footprint. These ancient symbols of kingly ritual can be found elsewhere in Argyll but historians see this print as highly significant. Tradition maintains it is the print of Fergus, first king of Dalriada. Excavations at the site have revealed metal-working remains, which, along with the numerous quern stones also found, suggests a fairly sizeable community was centred here.

CARNASSERIE CASTLE
Built by the zealous John Carswell, Carnasserie Castle was a suitably impressive home for the sixteenth-century churchman credited with reviving religion in Argyll and planting a minister in every west Argyll parish.

the Crinan Canal, brings the visitor to the fascinating area centred on Dunadd. This is no more than a rocky hillock suddenly rising out of the unexpected flatlands of the Crinan Moss or Moine Mhor (Gaelic: the big moor) where the River Add snakes its way down to its eventual lazy parallel course with the Crinan Canal. But it was here that the first Scots from Ireland chose as their stronghold in the sixth century. Thus it became the capital of ancient Dalriada. Strictly speaking, Dalriada was the name given to their homeland in Ireland by the tribe called the Scoti and they transferred it. This kingdom was eventually united with the territories of the Picts.

There are wide views from the hilltop and some rock-cut markings to puzzle over. There is the outline of a boar, a bowl cut into the rock, a mysterious inscription in the linear Celtic script known as ogam

Travelling north on the A816, ancient sites litter the landscape – look for signs to the Ri Cruin Cairn, the Temple Wood Stone Circle and the Nether Largie Burial Cairns, all in the Kilmartin Valley and dating from the Bronze Age, around 2-3000 BC. The fine collection of medieval graveslabs at Kilmartin Church seem positively modern by comparison.

Further north is Carnasserie Castle. Look for it west of the road, its foursquare tower rising above the trees. Built on the site of earlier forts on a dominating ridge overlooking the Kilmartin Valley, this large fortified sixteenth-century house is, in a sense, transitional in as far as it is one of the last tower houses built in Scotland. It shows innovative arrangements for a tower house as it has rooms laid out to connect with each other horizontally rather than vertically as was traditional in Scottish tower houses of that time.

Under the patronage of the Earl of Argyll, the castle was built from 1560 by the influential churchman John Carswell, who became the Bishop of the Isles in 1567. He is remembered for his translation of the *Reformed Church's Book of Common Order* (or *Knox's Liturgy*) into Gaelic, which set out the principles of Presbyterianism. This work was the first book ever printed in Gaelic.

At the head of Loch Craignish, an arm of the Firth of Lorn, a cul-de-sac road passes through the village of Ardfern with its yacht moorings. From the road end it is possible to continue on foot to Craignish Point. From a nearby hill, there are views of the Strait of Corryvreckan, famous for its whirlpool. Though about 4 miles (6.4 km) away, the roaring of the tide can be heard if the wind is westerly.

In typical Argyll fashion, the traveller journeys from ancient site to castle to garden – each so characteristic of the area. This is true of Kintyre, of Knapdale and also of the area the road now enters on its way north. This is the land of Lorn, stretching west from Loch Awe to the seaboard and the Firth of Lorn. A few

THE CRAIGNISH PENINSULA
A typical Argyll tangle of islands, looking west towards Shuna on the Craignish peninsula, one of many which make the seaboard a lifetime's exploration.

BALVICAR BAY, SEIL ISLAND
On the road to the 'Slate Islands' of Seil and Easdale. The islands were once a centre of slate quarrying, with records as far back as 1626. The industry came to an abrupt end after a flood in 1881.

minutes' drive to the north of Carnasserie, Arduaine Garden sits in a sheltered bowl on a small promontory hard by the sea edge between Loch Melfort and the Sound of Jura. In the care of the National Trust for Scotland, it is nationally renowned for its rhododendrons and azaleas, as well as its magnolias. Its waterside plants are also spectacular. The National Trust for Scotland take great pains to describe it as a plantsman's garden, rather than a tourist attraction – a quite subtle, if not slightly elitist, distinction.

Many visitors using Oban as a base make an excursion to the island of Seil, north of Arduaine by the main road. A single-arch bridge spans the 70-ft (21-m) wide tidal strait of Clachan Sound. This bridge, dating from 1791, is often called the Bridge over the Atlantic since it certainly spans at least some of that ocean's waters. Visit in summer and you may notice an attractive little pink-flowered plant growing on the bridge masonry. This is the fairy foxglove, an uncommon plant whose main home is in the mountains of southern Europe. It is a lover of lime-rich mortar.

Opposite the bridge is an inn called the Tigh na Truish, or Trousers House. It recalls the proscription of the kilt and tartan after the 1745 rebellion was put down. For nearly 40 years after, the wearing of Highland dress was banned. Highlanders in remoter parts would sometimes wear kilts at home but if travelling further afield would change at a convenient point, in this case, Trousers House.

Beyond the bridge, the exposed rock takes on a blue-grey, bedded look. Seil Island is one of what are known as the Slate Islands. Along with Easdale, it was a centre of slate quarrying for centuries, with written records going as far back as 1626. Nine million slates left the quarries at their peak in the mid nineteenth century. The industry came to an abrupt end in 1881 when a November storm flooded the workings.

The quarriers' cottages and the workings themselves fell into disrepair. However, the houses have been refurbished and various little businesses are putting something back into the local community. There is also a small museum on Easdale.

Further offshore are the Garvellach, the holy 'Isles of the Sea'. On these uninhabited little chips of land survive some of Britain's earliest ecclesiastical buildings, primitive cells and chapels, made with rough stones without mortar, and associated with St Columba and St Brendan. Under such conditions, the Celtic church survived the turmoil of Dark Age Europe.

EASDALE ISLAND

EASDALE ON SEIL ISLAND, with former slate-workers' cottages.

North and East of Oban

The area to the north and east of Oban has countless points of interest and comprises the classic touring grounds of Argyll, enjoyed by generations of visitors who have made Oban their base. There is spectacular scenery here in plenty: roadless Loch Etive, the even longer Loch Awe with its wooded islands, the long humped spine of Ben Cruachan and the views across Loch Linnhe to the wild hills of Ardgour all add to the grandeur of the area.

Just north of Oban, high on the battlements of Dunstaffnage Castle, is a good place to view the end of Ben Cruachan and glimpse the Connel Bridge spanning the Etive narrows. Built on a commanding rock with the sheltered anchorage of Dunstaffnage Bay nearby, this castle was a stronghold of the MacDougalls, the Lords of Lorn. The shape of its massive walling was dictated by the rock on which it stands, but the thirteenth-century masons' work has survived for more than 700 years remarkably intact. The castle was captured by Robert the Bruce in 1309. By 1470 it had been granted to the First Earl of Argyll. The remains of a finely wrought chapel of the thirteenth century stand nearby.

Continuing westward, the cantilever Connel Bridge soon dominates the view. Now a road bridge, which takes the main A828 north to Ballachulish and Glencoe, it was originally built to carry a railway branch line from Connel up to Ballachulish. The bridge was completed in 1903, the branch lasting till 1966. At the time of opening, only the Forth Bridge (in Britain) had a longer span. Immediately below the bridge is the odd phenomenon of the Falls of Lora, a kind of salt-water waterfall. Because of a lip of hard rock below the surface at the head of Loch Etive, on ebb tides, Loch Linnhe to the west drops faster,

DUNSTAFFNAGE CASTLE
The massive curtain walls of Dunstaffnage still stand almost 66 ft (20 m) high.

BEN CRUACHAN AND LOCH ETIVE (opposite). The summit ridge of Ben Cruachan is both long and complex.

CONNEL BRIDGE AND LOCH ETIVE
Connel Bridge was originally built as a railway bridge. It spans the narrows of Loch Etive, above the tidal confluence of the Falls of Lora.

parliament here in 1308 – the last, it is said, to conduct its business in Gaelic.

Many visitors stop at the Sea Life Centre on Loch Creran, with its displays of sea creatures from Scottish waters. Further to the north, Castle Stalker on its rocky islet presents the perfect foreground for the more distant panorama of the wild hills of Morven. The district of Appin starts on the north side of Loch Creran. The Highlands proper and the portals of Glencoe lie only a few miles further on.

Returning over the Connel Bridge, with the wild upper part of Loch Etive hidden from view, the main A85 leads on through woods and a narrow coastal farming strip to Taynuilt, where a sign leads down

creating a waterfall or cataract out of Loch Etive. On flood tides, the opposite happens, with sea water roaring noisily into Loch Etive. This curious event can be seen close by the main road at Connel.

Immediately beyond lies Benderloch, translated as 'the hill between two lochs', and the first views of the narrow island of Lismore out in Loch Linnhe. Lismore's prevailing rich green colour comes from its limestone, which has broken down to a fertile soil. Its name derives from the Gaelic meaning 'big garden'. Note that from here a little road leads down to the site of Ardchattan Priory. Robert the Bruce held a

to Bonawe. The broad-leaved woods are greatly admired today and treasured for their wildlife interest. In the eighteenth century they were an important resource and played a key part in the iron-smelting industry. In 1753, a smelting company moved its operations from England's Lake District to exploit the woodlands around Loch Etive. Haematite ore was shipped in from Cumbria, also in England. The Bonawe Iron Furnace consumed great quantities of timber in the form of charcoal. The buildings of the furnace complex, which comprise ore shed and charcoal sheds, as well as the furnace itself, have been

preserved by Historic Scotland, the government agency responsible for looking after a variety of historic sites in Scotland – not only castles and ancient monuments, but industrial features as well.

The charcoal itself was made by piling logs round a central stake on a rounded stance or level platform, about 25 ft (7.6 m) across. The resultant pile was covered in earth, the stake removed and the pile set alight. The slow-burning process took up to ten days.

These rounded platforms, often cut into hillsides now significantly bare of trees, can be found in several parts of the Highlands, for example, in Glen Nant on the B845, south of Bonawe, where there are also nature trails as part of a national nature reserve. Fortunately, tree cover still exists here.

East of Bonawe the main road runs into the gloomy Pass of Brander. In this steep-walled place Robert the Bruce defeated the Macdougalls in 1308.

CASTLE STALKER
A classic fortified Scottish tower house, Castle Stalker's backdrop includes the island of Lismore in the salt waters of Loch Linnhe.

KILCHURN CASTLE AND LOCH AWE
The Campbell stronghold overlooks Loch Awe, with Ben Lui in the distance.

They were kinsmen of the Red Comyn, a rival claimant to the Scottish throne whom Bruce had murdered. The rise of the Clan Campbell stems from the support of Bruce in this battle. They received the forfeited MacDougall lands and thereafter grew in power to play a significant role in Scotland's story as the Earls and later Dukes of Argyll.

The road, as it traverses the top end of the hammer-head of Loch Awe, is so close to the shoulders of mighty Ben Cruachan that they seem to all but overhang, giving no sense of the scale of this mighty horseshoe of cliff and crag. From viewpoints further south – from the gardens of the Ardanaiseig House Hotel, for example – the pale walls of a dam can be seen. This is the upper section of the Cruachan Pumped Storage Power Station. The lower section sits by the main road and can be visited.

In the Cruachan Power Station Visitor Centre the intricacies of hydro-electric power are explained – how the water stored in a dam high in a corrie about 1200 ft (365.8 m) up the mountain powers turbines on its way down to Loch Awe, then is pumped back up again at off-peak times. Visitors also have the option of being taken more than half a mile (1 km) into the mountain by minibus right down to the turbine hall: a unique experience and sometimes one of the few midge-free places in all of Argyll in late summer.

Loch Awe is at least 24 miles (39 km) long, making it the longest loch in Scotland. Kilchurn Castle sits at its easternmost tip on a rocky outcrop just above water level. Even from its battlements there is little more than a hint of the loch's gently winding nature. However, the panoramas from this ancient Campbell stronghold are truly glorious and well worth the walk across the river flats from the car park off the A85.

Whatever the angle, the ragged walls and towers of Kilchurn are a powerful visual symbol of Highland Scotland. They have long been used in Scottish guide-books and promotional literature – the very essence of the nation's martial past, framed by grand mountains and reflected in the waters of a sombre loch. Sir Colin Campbell of Glenorchy built the original tower house in the fifteenth century. The accommodation was extended by John, First Earl of Breadalbane in the seventeenth century, by way of barrack ranges built out from the original tower. The political machi-nations of the Campbells required the maintenance of a militia and hence the accommodation but

by the latter half of the eighteenth century more peaceable times resulted in the abandonment of the fortress.

If the views from the battlements here are worth seeing, there is yet one place more where visual splendour is all. Only a mile or two further east on the A85 is the little settlement of Dalmally. An old road runs south-west from the village, formerly joining today's road to Inveraray. At its end and highest point sits a curious circular object, built with grey stone, like a temple. This is the Duncan Ban Macintyre Monument. Macintyre (1742-1812) has been described as the best-loved of the eighteenth-century Gaelic poets, meaning that his work remains a closed book to most Scots today. His body of work included songs of praise to Campbell chiefs, drinking songs, satires and countryside poems. His most famous work is 'In Praise of Ben Doran', dating from the 1750s. It is not only Robert Burns who has memorials in Scotland – in fact, Macintyre is sometimes known as the 'Burns of the Highlands'. In an area noted for its fine views, his monument commands amongst the finest of them, from Ben Lui in the east to the soaring tops of Ben Cruachan in the west.

LOCH AWE is Scotland's longest loch at around 24 miles (39 km). Steamer services formerly operated between the villages of Lochawe at the northern end and Ford in the south.

Oban

The Norsemen who knew this seaboard so well had a word for a sheltered lagoon or bay in which boats could be taken ashore for the winter. This was an 'ob', which along with a Gaelic diminutive ending make the word Oban. The sheltered bay is still the key to Oban today.

When Boswell and Johnson visited in 1773, there was only one 'tolerable inn' in what was then still a small village. Oban's development as a tourism resort followed on soon after. Just one element in the story was the Welsh travel writer Thomas Pennant's *Tour in Scotland and a Voyage to the Hebrides* which appeared soon afterwards. It made the general public aware of the wonders of the then recently discovered island of Staffa with its basalt columns. To this day, Staffa remains on the cruise options which Oban can offer as a kind of Hebridean gateway. By 1812 Scotland's first steamship *Comet* had called, the herald for generations of steamers and cruisers which put Oban firmly on the tourist map, along with the arrival of the railway in 1880.

Solid Victorian frontages and lots of sturdy villas

and hotels are the first impressions of 'downtown' Oban, which still bustles in the main season as a natural route centre. The first railway company here described it in its advertising material as 'The Charing Cross of the Highlands'. The MacDougalls of Dunstaffnage, the local proprietors, had forbidden the entry of the railway directly from the east over their land, so it had to sneak in by a back way, via Glen Cruten south of the town. As a result today's waterfront and long crescent of a promenade add much to the attractiveness of the setting, instead of having a railway running along it (as happened at Fort William, Oban's northern rival).

Yet another conspicuous feature of the town dominates the horizon from many angles. At the beginning of the twentieth century, McCaig's Folly, or McCaig's Tower, echoing the Coliseum, was built on a prominent site overlooking the town by a local banker as a kind of 'job creation' scheme for local unemployed stone masons. He built it as a memorial to his family and it was intended to have a museum and art gallery within it, plus a central tower 100 ft (30.5 m) high. Unfortunately (or otherwise) after the death of the philanthropic banker, his plans were never completed.

McCaig's Tower makes an excellent viewpoint over the bay, as does Pulpit Hill at the south end of the town. From here the sheltered anchorage, protected by the island of Kerrera from the full force of the westerlies, can be fully appreciated.

Today's Oban offers a good range of shops for its guests, as well as plenty of evening entertainments in its hotels and local halls. Other visitor attractions include A World in Miniature which displays handcrafted miniature rooms and furniture made in a tiny scale. Oban Distillery and a glassware factory can also be visited.

Historical sites include the remaining fragment of Dunollie Castle, a former MacDougall stronghold, on a crag at the end of the promenade on the way to Oban's own little beach.

The island of Kerrera, sheltering Oban Bay and connected by ferry from Gallanach, is sometimes overlooked by Oban's visitors. It is a fertile and farmed island with a series of raised beaches on the eastern side. Its western coastline has little habitation. In 1249, King Alexander II died on the island, while campaigning to wrest the Hebrides from Norse control, a fact recalled by the name Dalrigh, the king's field, just south of the island's ferry quay.

OBAN HARBOUR
As well as a ferry terminal, Oban is also a commercial fishing port. McCaig's Tower is conspicuous on the skyline.

Not only is it large, in Hebridean terms, but it has great beauty and a strong sense of solitude and emptiness, in spite of a wave of new settlements from other parts of Britain. It has a history of emigration and eviction from the eighteenth century onward. Today, its tourist industry brings many thousands of visitors not only to enjoy its wild scenery but in particular to cross the Ross of Mull to Iona, cradle of Scottish Christianity and ancient burial site of the kings of Scotland.

Grandeur and emptiness together create a variety of habitats. Mull is especially noted for the richness of its wildlife and has a number of specialities. It is, for example, best known, amongst wildlife watchers, for the abundance and variety of its birds of prey. Buzzards perch on roadside telegraph poles and fence posts whilst the elusive golden eagle and re-introduced white-tailed sea eagle can often be seen soaring over the cliffs to the west of the island or above the upland habitat of the south and west. Peregrines can also be spotted in these areas. Hen harriers and short-eared owls hunt over young coniferous plantations and sparrowhawks frequent the

Mull & Iona

DUART CASTLE, MULL
The early chiefs of the Clan Maclean chose Duart as their seat for its commanding views of the sea-lanes of the Firth of Lorn and the Sound of Mull.

Mull derives its name from a Gaelic word meaning a high, wide tableland. Its main feature is the stepped appearance of its ancient lava flows, worn and eroded into spectacular terracing, notably in the west around the sea lochs of Loch na Keal and Loch Tuath. It is a large enough island on the western seaboard to be noted on the famous map of the Egyptian map-maker and geographer Ptolemy in the second century AD, where it was called Maleus.

more mature woodlands.

Another draw is the marine mammals off its coasts. Because of the indented nature of the island's shore, Mull has around 300 miles (482.8 km) of coastline. Grey seals (breeding on the Treshnish Isles offshore – see page 57) can be seen, from the roadside, basking on inshore rocks at places such as Salen and Burg. Lucky visitors can occasionally surprise unsuspecting otters at play. One of the most delightful mammals to watch, the otter spends much of its time amongst the wrack-covered rocks at the water's edge – a habitat which exists along much of Mull's shoreline.

Most visitors arrive at Craignure by way of Oban, though of its two other mainland ferry connections, one links Tobermory and Ardnamurchan and the other crosses from Lochaline to Fishnish, a little west of Craignure. The Mull ferries provide a foretaste of the wildlife diversity with Manx shearwater, storm petrel, guillemot, razorbill and black guillemot breeding on offshore islands to the west and usually to be noted en route to and from the mainland, along with sooty shearwater, arctic and great skuas.

Craignure, the ferry terminal, is within easy reach of Mull's two best-known castles, Torosay and Duart. Torosay Castle can be reached by a narrow-gauge railway – the only one of its kind on a Scottish island – which takes 20 minutes to run from close by the pier at Craignure to the castle grounds. Scottish baronial in style, Torosay has a very friendly air, and much of this family home is accessible to visitors. There are plenty of good-humoured, idiosyncratic information boards and informal family albums, for example. Nineteen life-size Venetian statues are

important features of the terraced garden. The building only dates from the 1850s, and was designed by David Bruce, while the garden is turn-of-the-century by Sir David Lorimer.

From Torosay, there is a shore walk to Duart Castle as well as road access. This ancient seat dates in part from the thirteenth century and commands the approaches of the Sound of Mull from the south. Originally built by the Macdougalls, it was in Maclean hands by the fourteenth century. It was ruined by the Campbells in 1691, but bought and restored by Sir Fitzroy Maclean in 1911.

Continuing on an island circuit, grey rocks and vivid green grass are the dominant colours of the interior, especially in Glen More with its high rock-faces. These stepped terraces of ancient lava-flows

BEN MORE, MULL
At 3169 ft (966 m) Ben More is the only island mountain (outside Skye) to be classified as a Munro.

*IONA ABBEY
Between the sixth
and eighth centuries
this remote Christian
community profoundly
influenced religious
life in Scotland and
was one of the most
important centres of
the Celtic Church.*

reach their highest point in Ben More, the only island 'Munro' (Scottish mountain over 3000 ft (914 m) outside Skye. The Ross of Mull, a wide promontory with scattered settlements, gives good views of the dramatic cliffs of Ardmeanach, the shorter promontory to the north.

The Glen More road runs west to reach Loch Scridain. Near its head another road goes down to the remote south coast. From the little pierhead at the tiny settlement of Carsaig a very rough path goes west, below lava cliffs, to the impressive Carsaig Arches – though this is a long excursion only for the fit and agile. It shares this feature with The Burg, on another very rugged stretch of coast on the north side of Loch Scridain. A long walk in is needed to reach the feature, a 40-million-year-old fossil tree set into a cliff, known as McCulloch's Tree. While Ardmeanach is the name given to the area north of Loch Scridain, part of it is

known locally as the Wilderness. The Burg is in the care of the National Trust for Scotland.

The road on the stretch north of Loch Scridain round the west side of Mull is spectacular. It cuts through stepped cliffs and drops to the shores of Loch Keal, whose name derives from the Gaelic for the loch of cliffs, an entirely apt description. This stretch of the road, which has an occasional scattering of fallen splinters of rock from the heights above, has a very remote flavour, with views west to a dramatic coastline and east to the screes of Ben More. However, a few rocks on the road are nothing compared to the local tale here which recounts how a huge rock, still to be seen today near Gribun, landed on a cottage in which a couple were staying on their wedding night, destroying the building and the luckless occupants.

Further on, there are fine views of the island of Ulva guarding Loch na Keil. This island was visited by

Johnson and Boswell on their Hebridean tour. It was the birthplace of Lachlan MacQuarrie (1761-1824), known as the 'Father of Australia' because under his energetic administrations and firm rule while he was Governor of New South Wales the young nation grew so much in prosperity.

Dramatic seascapes last until Calgary Bay is reached with its gleaming white sands and pocket-sized strip of machair, the shell-sand pasture characteristic of the Western Isles. It is often said that the town of Calgary in Canada was given its name by the original inhabitants who were cleared from the vicinity in 1822 – look in the bracken near the old pier for the ruins of the townships here. In fact, the Canadian settlement was given its name much later by a Colonel MacLeod of the Royal North-West Mounted Police and recalls Calgary House, in the trees above the bay, which he had visited on holiday in 1883.

A gentler landscape leads on to Dervaig, where the Old Byre Heritage Centre presents the history of the island. Nearby is the Mull Little Theatre which offers a varied programme and claims the distinction of being the smallest professional theatre in the UK. Further on, the main town of Tobermory was founded as a fishing station in 1787, though it gradually declined after the railway arrived at Oban and attracted the traffic. The brightly painted crescent of mainly eighteenth-century buildings gives Tobermory a very attractive air.

As originally conceived the commercial premises were on the waterfront, with the fishermen's houses on the terrace above, the whole layout being dictated by the narrowness of the frontage and the steep rise to

IONA
Even without its religious significance, Iona has an idyllic quality. The Ross of Mull beyond the Sound of Iona provides the backdrop to this typically Hebridean beach.

LOCH TUATH, MULL
Looking over Loch Tuath on Mull's west coast towards the islands of Gometra and Ulva, which are joined to each other by a bridge.

for the lucky diver.

Allow at least a couple of days if you intend to circumnavigate Mull by road – much longer if you intend to explore or get to grips with its rugged landscapes.

At the end of the promontory of the Ross of Mull lies the island of Iona, reached from Fionnphort. Though Iona is only 3 miles (4.8 km) long, much parking space is necessary at the Mull side because of the popularity of the island, on which visitors will not need cars. The ferry service is frequent in the summer. Iona is in the care of the National Trust for Scotland.

the upper part of the town. The place is also associated with a sunken galleon from the Spanish armada. Said to be the *Almirante de Florencia*, she called in at the bay seeking provisions. The local legend recounts how after taking stores from a Donald MacLean he had to come aboard to ask for payment, whereupon he was locked up. He managed to escape but started a fire while doing so. The ship blew up and its scanty remains are scattered in the silty bay. Cannon have been retrieved in the past and local tales speak of a fortune in Spanish gold – 30 million ducats – waiting

The Irish monk Columba chose Iona for the setting up of a monastery in AD 563 because it was the first place he landed from which Ireland could not be seen – or so the story goes. Christianity was actually brought to Scotland first by St Ninian in 397 but the word of St Columba's church was spread widely amongst the northern Picts, so that Iona is often described as the cradle of Scottish Christianity. The religious settlement was the burial place of the kings of Scotland till the eleventh century. Forty-eight are said to lie here, from Fergus MacEric in the sixth century to Macbeth in the eleventh century. The Norsemen sacked the settlement repeatedly and most of the community was transferred to Kells in Ireland. Though some monks stayed on over the generations, the site finally fell into disuse around the time of the Reformation. Restoration work began at the turn of the twentieth century, the Iona Community was founded in 1938 and today the restored buildings are a spiritual centre under the Kirk of Scotland.

Near the abbey stands the earliest building on the site, St Oran's Chapel, associated with St Margaret, the eleventh-century Queen of King Malcolm Canmore. Early Christian crosses also survive, including the most complete cross, that of St Martin, decorated with religious scenes and dating from the eighth century.

Beyond the restored cloisters, the most mystifying aspect is how the little island still feels peaceful in spite of all the visitors. Most folk only make the short walk from the ferry pier via the thirteenth-century nunnery to the abbey. However, the rest of the island has much character and memorable beauty. There is a good beach on the east side beyond Sligineach, on the Sound of Mull. Beyond that, an old marble quarry marks the site of an industry carried out sporadically for centuries until final closure in 1914. Look for the green serpentine pebbles, naturally polished by wave action in the bays at the extreme south of the island.

There is flowery machair land in the west and, just to the south of these shell sand pastures, a spouting cave, spectacular at certain states of the tide. At the other end of the island there are some fine stretches of white sand, which a walk to the top of Dun I will reveal. This is the highest point on Iona at 332 ft

(101 m) so is hardly in the demanding category of hillwalking but makes an excellent viewpoint.

From this high point, look also for Erraid island, lying close inshore to the south, difficult to see separately from Mull itself. It is separated from Mull only by a stretch of sand at low tide, a fact which Robert Louis Stevenson wove into his adventure story *Kidnapped*, after David Balfour, the hero of the tale, survived the wreck of the brig *Covenant*. From a famous lighthouse engineering family, Stevenson knew the area well and in his tale bends local geography only a little, moving the Torran Rocks – a treacherous reef some miles south of Iona and on which the fictional vessel foundered – within swimming distance of Erraid, enabling Balfour to get ashore.

TOBERMORY HARBOUR
Tobermory is associated with the sinking of a ship from the Spanish armada, reputedly laden with gold. Though the sinking is historical fact, it seems probable that the treasure is simply a legend.

Staffa

FINGAL'S CAVE, STAFFA

Located between the Treshnish Isles and Iona, the cooling of lava formed these famous basalt pillars.

If any evidence were needed of the sheer remoteness in former days of the Hebridean Islands it is the fact that Fingal's Cave, indeed, the island of Staffa, was not actually recorded until 1772. The discovery was made by the explorer Joseph Banks who described the island of Staffa, off the coast of Mull, as one of the greatest natural curiosities in the world, 'The Giant's Causeway in Ireland, or Stonehenge in England, are but trifles when compared to this island'.

Thus Banks was duly impressed by the basalt columns. To be accurate, the island was known to the Vikings who gave it its name, literally staff-island because of the columnar rock formations. There is also the curious tale that the town of Stäfa on lake Zurich in Switzerland was named after the island by a visiting monk from Iona, who obviously travelled widely. The most famous site on the island became known as Fingal's Cave, after the legendary Celtic hero. The island even had steamers regularly viewing it, sailing from Oban as early as the 1820s. It was visited by a procession of heavyweight Romantics thereafter: Wordsworth, Keats and Scott from the world of literature; the artists Turner and Daniell; most notably Mendelssohn in 1829 whose visit inspired the *Hebrides Overture,* usually known as 'Fingal's Cave'. Even Queen Victoria called in 1847, managing to sail into the cave, the weather being exceptionally calm. Wordsworth records how his visit was spoiled by the large crowds of tourists – in 1833. The island has not had a resident population since 1800.

In geological terms the extraordinary rock formations were caused by the slow cooling of lava to form hexagonal (sometimes pentagonal) columns. It is worth noting that there are other rock features and caves to see as well as Fingal's Cave, with such names as the Wishing Chair, the Causeway – recalling the Giant's Causeway in Ulster – the Colonnade and Clamshell Cave, so called because the entrance columns are twisted in spectacular whorls like a shell.

Today, there is still a choice of excursions from Oban and Mull which go to the island, one of the most romantic sites in all of the Hebrides, though landing is only possible in calm conditions. Staffa is owned by the National Trust for Scotland. The Trust were given the island by a wealthy New Yorker, John Elliott, who bought it in 1986 as a novel birthday present for his wife and then made the donation.

The Treshnish Isles

The remains of the great lava sheets which make up the western headlands of the north part of Mull also form Staffa and the Treshnish Isles. Conspicuous on the horizon from Mull all along the shores of Loch Tuath, the lonely little Treshnish group has seen no permanent habitation since 1834. Summer occupation continued for a further few years. The islands have an exposed aspect to weather from the south-west in particular and there are strong tides around them. There are no safe anchorages and landing depends entirely on weather. One of the tiniest, Cairn na Burgh More, at the northern end, was formerly fortified. Its defences were destroyed in 1504, in a campaign against the Lords of the Isles, by royalist forces under the Earl of Arran.

The Treshnish Isles' distinct shape, mostly table-topped and surrounded by low-ish cliffs, reflects their volcanic origins. The largest island, Lunga, has a terraced appearance, where the lava flows lie over one another. Bac Mor (Gaelic: the big hump) is even more distinctive, with its hill in the centre of an otherwise flat island giving rise to its usual name of the Dutchman's Cap. These islands are the breeding ground of auks, Manx shear-waters and storm petrels, and a pupping ground for grey seals.

LUNGA, one of the Treshnish Isles.

PUFFINS and other sea birds flourish on Lunga.

57

Coll

Though geographically near Mull, the islands of Coll and Tiree have strong echoes of the Western Isles, especially in the extent of the machair, the limy shell-sand flower-flecked grasslands of the coast. The machair of Coll is found along the windward edges of the western and southern coasts. At places like Hogh Bay, on the west coast, the sand has been blown into dunes, then knitted together by bents grass. Facing the Atlantic rollers is a magnificent beach, its empty sandy tidelines the undisturbed haunt of wading birds and gulls. Similarly, there are well-developed dunes between Breachacha and Caolis. The Royal Society for the Protection of Birds has a reserve here in the west end,

which is of prime importance for corncrakes, a summer visitor in sharp decline because of intensive farming methods practised throughout much of Britain, except for the Hebridean islands. After they arrive from Africa in May, they hide in tall vegetation like yellow irises before moving into tall grass to nest. Because of their late nesting on the ground, their nests are habitually destroyed by the cutting for hay and silage. Traditional Hebridean practice is to cut late, giving the birds a better chance of survival. Both on Coll and Tiree the RSPB encourages corncrake-friendly farming practices.

In contrast to the green richness of the south-western end, much of the rest of Coll is composed of acid rock lying near the surface, so that peat and thin

moorland have developed. Trees shelter and cluster near dwellings – otherwise the island is mostly treeless.

Historically, the island belonged to Maclean of Coll. This line of chieftains, enlightened for their time, had talents both as soldiers and bards. They had a strong interest in the arts, as patrons of pipers and harpists. Most significantly, the thirteenth chief ensured the island clansmen were kept out of the 1745 rebellion. He later received a special royal dispensation which prevented him from becoming a vassal of the Campbells. By 1840, the population stood at around 1400, with one-third of this number being directly supported by the laird as the land could not provide enough to sustain this population. Subsequently – and drastically – it was cleared in the 1850s to make way for dairy farmers from Ayrshire, so that even today the island is mostly farmed, rather than crofted. In fact, in the period 1841-1951 Coll lost 85% of its population.

The absence of a really safe harbour on Coll has always hindered the development of a local fishing industry.

There are two castles at Breachacha, the old castle being a fifteenth-century tower house once under the control of the Lords of the Isles, while the new is a mid eighteenth-century mansion. The English lexicographer and man of letters, Doctor Johnson, stayed here during his famous 1773 Hebridean journey with his Scottish guide Boswell. The main centre of population today is around Arinagour, where the ferry calls.

BREACHACHA CASTLE, COLL

ARINAGOUR, Coll's main centre of population.

Tiree

TIREE
in midsummer evening light. Looking across from Balephetrish Hill to Gott, the Treshnish Isles and distant Mull.

Tiree, Coll's neighbour, has a more populated look, with a crofting tradition stretching back about 200 years. At around 750 people it has five times the resident population of Coll. Its machair and windblown grassland is extensive, its main colours the emerald green of pasture and the dazzling blue of sea and sky. Tiree, some say, means 'the land of corn' – a reference to its fertility in Gaelic – and certainly, the overwhelming impression is of its low greenness. The agricultural regime on the island is mostly concerned with cattle and sheep, though with some grass and cereal production, when livestock is put on to the communal pastures on moor and machair.

The early history of Tiree is hinted at by the finds at island's broch which included tools and pottery dating from around 800 BC. St Columba is also associated with the island. His cousin, Baitheine, had founded a religious settlement at Sorobaidh and Columba had occasion to visit him. Sailing into Gott Bay, he struck a rock which all but sunk his fragile vessel. Local legend says that he cursed the rock – a tradition, apparently, still followed by today's sailors.

The island's monastery was of some importance and is also associated with St Comgall, a Pictish affiliate of St Columba.

Tiree is sometimes also called in Gaelic the land lower than the waves. Because of this low profile it does not catch the clouds and rain off the Atlantic and instead has earned a reputation for statistically high average sunshine hours, notably in May and June. A 30-year average gives it a figure of around six-and-a-half hours daily in June.

Like Coll, Tiree also has a reputation for being windswept. Some of the surviving older dwelling houses on the island (the traditional black houses) still show the modifications which the builders used to defy the wind. Walls are thick – up to 9 ft (2.7 m) on the windward side in some houses – and of double-skinned construction, the space between being filled with sand into which the rainwater ran from the roof. The roofs themselves are low not just because of the lack of local timber but also the low profile offers less wind resistance. The winds on the island practically inhibit tree-growth. However these Atlantic breezes

also whip up the sea into spectacular breakers and provide the conditions much appreciated by surfers: the island regularly hosts international competitions.

As well as surfers, Tiree also attracts birdwatchers. It is also, like Coll, a stronghold of the corncrake. Today's visitors are not that likely to spot a corncrake, so skulking and secretive is the bird in cover. However, it betrays its presence by a persistent call, especially at night – and most birdwatchers are happy just to hear it. It has a foothold on the fertile sward of Tiree, where

BALEPHETRISH, TIREE
The fertile land of the island lends itself to agriculture, which is mostly concerned with cattle and sheep. Tiree has a resident population of about 750 people.

CROFT HOUSE, SANDAIG MUSEUM, TIREE

BALEPHUIL BAY, TIREE (opposite). A typical dazzling shell-sand beach backed by a settlement on the machair, in the south-west corner of Tiree.

with a commanding view. A broch is a circular double-walled structure shaped like an upturned flowerpot in profile, and highly characteristic of coastal regions of the north and west. In general they are thought to have been built as protection against sea-borne raiders around 2000 years ago. The Tiree broch, whose walls survive to about 7 ft (2 m) in height, is thought to have been re-modelled a couple of centuries after construction as a non-defensive round house and, later still, intermittently used for settlement or shelter. A bone comb of the Viking Age was found on the site.

Tiree also has two museums. The Sandaig Thatched House Museum opens in the summer months and is furnished in period to give a flavour of island life at the beginning of the twentieth century. The Skerryvore Lighthouse Museum is in Hynish in the former Signalling Tower. This was used as a shore base for, and to communicate with, the Skerryvore Lighthouse which stands 12 miles (19.3 km) offshore, before the days of radio.

However, visitors mostly come to Coll and Tiree for the leisurely and peaceful air of islands out in the western sea. The islands attract birdwatchers, botanists, surfers and anyone with a taste for the rhythm of Hebridean life, dictated by tides and the ferry timetable.

the RSPB is encouraging agricultural techniques which provide the necessary grassy cover which corncrakes require for successful rearing of their chicks.

Elsewhere, the dunes and machair are also of interest because Tiree has no rabbits and in consequence they have a particularly lush look, except where they have been over-grazed by cattle and sheep. The grasslands around Barrapol and Ballevullin in the south-west are particularly good for a variety of lime-loving wildflowers.

The island's main prehistoric site is Dun Mor at Vaul, the remains of a broch, perched on a rocky knoll

INDEX

Entries in **bold** *indicate pictures*

First published in Great Britain in 1998 by Lomond Books, 36 West Shore Road, Granton, Edinburgh, EH5 1QD
Produced by Colin Baxter Photography Ltd

Photographs Copyright © Colin Baxter 1998
Text Copyright © Colin Baxter Photography Ltd 1998
All rights reserved

No part of this book may be reproduced, stored in a retrieval system or transmitted in
any form or by any means without prior written permission of the publishers.

A CIP catalogue record for this book is available from the British Library

ISBN 0-947782 76-1

Printed in Hong Kong

Front cover photograph: *KYLES OF BUTE* Back cover photograph: *IONA BEACH & ROSS OF MULL*
Page 1 photograph: *STANDING STONES NEAR KILMARTIN*